# GALILEO IN 90 MINUTES

920

John and Mary Gribbin

# GALILEO
(1564–1642)
## in 90 minutes

Constable · London

First published in Great Britain 1997
by Constable and Company Limited
3 The Lanchesters, 162 Fulham Palace Road
London W6 9ER
Copyright © John and Mary Gribbin 1997
The right of John and Mary Gribbin to be identified
as authors of this work has been asserted by them
in accordance with the Copyright,
Designs and Patents Act 1988
ISBN 0 09 477110 3
Set in Linotype Sabon by
Rowland Phototypesetting Ltd,
Bury St Edmunds, Suffolk
Printed in Great Britain by
St Edmundsbury Press Ltd,
Bury St Edmunds, Suffolk

A CIP catalogue record for this book
is available from the British Library

# Contents

# Galileo in context

Galileo Galilei was the founding father of the scientific investigation of the world, and it is appropriate that he should always be known by his given name, Galileo, just as the man who put rock 'n' roll on the map is always known simply as Elvis. In their respective fields, each was 'the King'.

In fact, Galileo owed both his first and his last name to an illustrious ancestor. The family name had been Bonaiuti until the middle of the fifteenth century, when it was changed to Galilei in honour of Galileo Bonaiuti, an eminent physician and magistrate in whose glory his descendants were eager to bask. 'Our' Galileo was born just over a hundred years after his eponymous ancestor died. The great Italian artist Michelangelo died in the same month that Galileo was born; later that year, 1564, William Shakespeare was born at Stratford-upon-Avon. Columbus had discovered America just 72 years previously, and Galileo would be 56 years old when the *Mayflower* carried the Pilgrim Fathers to New England.

The world was changing in the second half

of the sixteenth century, but one aspect of the world had scarcely changed for more than a thousand years. In science, the ultimate authority (indeed, virtually the *only* authority) was Aristotle, the Greek philosopher who had lived in the fourth century BC. Aristotle (who, among other things, was the tutor of the boy prince who grew up to become Alexander the Great) was an extremely influential figure in Greek philosophy, and later in Roman philosophy, but his pervasive influence in sixteenth-century Europe owed much to a chain of accidents.

After the fall of Rome, most of Aristotle's works were lost to European civilization. But they survived in Byzantium, capital of the Eastern Roman Empire, and there the Greek texts were translated first into Syriac, then from Syriac into Arabic. In their Arabic form they were brought to the attention of European scholars via the spread of Islam (which had reached Spain by the eighth century AD), and were translated into Latin in the twelfth and thirteenth centuries. As you can imagine, the Latin versions were very scrambled after all these wanderings, but the interest they aroused led to the rediscovery of the original

Greek texts in Byzantium (by then known as Constantinople, and today as Istanbul). New translations were made from Greek directly into Latin – then the universal language of European scholars – at the instigation of Thomas Aquinas.

All these wanderings were, in a way, appropriate. Aristotle himself used to teach his students while walking about, and as a result his followers (literally) became known as 'Peripatetics', a name which was still used in Galileo's time. Unfortunately, far from being the free-and-easy kind of discipline that such a name conjures up, Aristotelianism was both rigid and wrong.

The really bad thing about Aristotelianism was that it was based on the notion that the truth about the world could be determined by pure thought – philosophy – without actually carrying out tests (what we would now call experiments) to see if the theories and hypotheses were right. Thus, for example, according to the Peripatetics (but translating into modern units), a heavier object would fall faster than a lighter object. Specifically, an object weighing 100 kilograms would fall 100 metres in the same time it took for an object weighing 1 kilogram to fall 1 metre, both of them starting from rest. The blindingly obvious fact that this could be tested by dropping two objects with different weights at the same time simply did not come into it.

Aristotle believed that the Sun, stars and other heavenly bodies were perfect and unchanging (among other things, this meant they were perfectly spherical), that the Earth was at the centre of the Universe, and that the Sun, Moon, planets and stars were carried round the Earth in perfect circles by crystalline spheres to which they were attached. None of this seemed crazy in the fourth century BC, but it became set in stone because the Peripatetics simply refused to test their ideas by experimenting, or to take any notice of the results of other people's experiments. Aristotle's picture was modified in detail, principally by Claudius Ptolemy in the second century AD, who introduced the idea of 'epicycles': each planet orbited in a tiny circle, the centre of which orbited the Earth.

When those Greek texts were translated into Latin by the monks working under the orders of Thomas Aquinas, they struck a chord with the Catholic Church. Aristotle's idea of *geometrical* perfection (which had nothing at all to do with religion) harmonized, in the eyes of Thomas Aquinas, with the idea of the perfection of God and of God's works. So the whole kit and caboodle of Aristotelian cosmology was swallowed up wholesale by the Church. Henceforth, to question any of this stuff would be to question the perfection of God, and would therefore be heresy.

This was the situation when Galileo came on the scene. Cheaply printed books (and pamphlets) had begun to be available early in the sixteenth century, spreading knowledge outside the traditional centres of the monasteries and the Church-dominated universities. Thinkers such as Nicholas Copernicus and Tycho Brahe had begun to question the received wisdom, from their relatively safe positions in northern Europe – not too close to Rome. But in the formal centres of learning, the party line held firm. The role of the professors of natural philosophy (as science was then called) was not to test the Universe to find out how it worked, but to preserve the Aristotelian tradition, and make sure that students learned it in just the same way that the professors had learned it when they had been students.

But Galileo had a head start on the other students. His father, Vincenzio, was an accomplished professional musician (a respected calling then) and keenly interested in mathematics and musical theory. In his *Dialogue of Ancient and Modern Music*, published just when Galileo went off to university, he wrote:

> It appears to me that they who in proof of any assertion rely simply on the weight of authority, without adducing any argument [that is, experimental evidence] in support of it, act very absurdly.

Nothing could be more anti-establishment and anti-Aristotelian. Vincenzio could get away with it in the world of music, though even there his ideas caused a stir. His son, brought up to question authority and find things out for himself, would find it harder to get away with such ideas when it came to discussing the place of the Earth in the Universe.

# Life and work

Galileo was born on 15 February 1564 in Pisa, in the Tuscany region of northwest Italy, a centre of the Renaissance. The town, ruled by the Duke of Florence, Cosimo de' Medici, was flourishing and prosperous. Cosimo himself would be crowned Duke of Tuscany by the Pope in 1570, as a reward for his military campaigns against the Moors.

Galileo was the eldest of seven children (his father, Vincenzio, and mother, Giulia, had married in 1562), but the only ones we know anything about are his sister Virginia, born in 1573, brother Michelangelo, born in 1575, and another sister, Livia, born in 1587. The others, a boy and two girls, may have died in infancy. Vincenzio came originally from Florence (he was born there in 1520), from a respected family now slightly less affluent than in previous generations, but still very much part of respectable society. In 1572 he returned to Florence to re-establish himself there. His wife and younger children went with him, but Galileo stayed in Pisa with one of his mother's relatives for a while, and joined them in 1574, when he was 10. There may have been some plan for Galileo to learn the wool trade, which was the relative's business; if so, nothing came of it.

In Florence, the family moved in high circles. Although never wealthy, Vincenzio was a court musician and mixed with dukes and princes. And Florence was the capital of Tuscany, the very centre of the Renaissance, then at the height of its fame as the intellectual heart of Europe.

Until he was 11, Galileo was educated privately at home, by his father and the occasional tutor. He developed an aptitude for the lute (his father's favourite instrument) and reached professional standard, and although he only played for amusement the instrument remained a source of pleasure throughout his life. In 1575 the boy was sent away for more formal education, to the monastery at Vallombroso, in the mountains 30 kilometres east of Florence.

He liked the way of life there so much that at the age of 15 he joined the order as a novice. His horrified anti-establishment father extracted him from the clutches of the monks on the pretext of taking him to see a doctor about an eye infection. The infection was

genuine, and so was the doctor, but what Vincenzio didn't mention was that he had no
intention of bringing the boy back. Although
Galileo's studies continued in Florence under
the supervision of the same order of monks,
he lived at home where his father could keep
him clear of any indoctrination.

Vincenzio was keen to see his eldest son
established in a respectable and financially
rewarding career, and intended him to
become a physician, like his ancestral name-
sake. So in 1581 Galileo was enrolled as a
medical student at the University of Pisa. To
keep his expenses down, he lodged with the
same relative, Muzio Tedaldi, who had
looked after him for a couple of years when
he was a child. Almost immediately, he established a reputation as an awkward student
who was not afraid to question established
ideas, and earned the nickname of 'the
wrangler'.

Much later in life, he wrote of his first formal encounter with Aristotelian ideas, and
how he had immediately thought of a refu-
tation of the idea that objects of different
weights fall at different speeds. He had seen
with his own eyes that hailstones of very

different sizes and weights reach the ground together in a storm. According to the Peripatetics, that could mean only that the heavier hailstones had started their journeys higher in the clouds – *exactly* the right amount higher to ensure that they arrived at the ground with their lighter counterparts. To the young Galileo, it made more sense to argue that all the hailstones had started in the same cloud layer, and fallen at the same speed.

But this wasn't what he was supposed to be concerned with: it had nothing to do with the study of medicine. His career was turned around early in 1583, during his second year of medical studies, when Galileo met Ostilio Ricci, the court mathematician of the Grand Duke of Tuscany. The whole court took up residence in Pisa each year from Christmas to Easter, which was how Galileo got to know Ricci socially. It was only by accident that he called on his new friend when Ricci was giving a lecture to some students, and stayed to listen, fascinated by the subject. It was Galileo's first contact with mathematics (as distinct from basic arithmetic), and he was hooked. He sat in on other lectures by Ricci, and began to study Euclid instead of his medical textbooks.

Ricci was sufficiently impressed by Galileo's quick grasp of the subject to back him up when he asked Vincenzio for permission to abandon his medical studies and become a mathematician. Knowing how limited the job opportunities for mathematicians were, Vincenzio refused, but Galileo continued to study mathematics anyway. The result was that he left the university in 1585 without a degree of any kind, and went back to Florence, where he tried to make a living by giving private tuition in mathematics and natural philosophy.

It was probably at Pisa that Galileo made one of his most profound observations. According to legend, it was while he was watching a swinging chandelier in the cathedral, during a rather dull sermon, that he realized that the pendulum always took the same time for one swing, whether it swung through a long arc or a short one (he timed the swing using his own pulse). He immediately rushed home, carried out a series of experiments with pendulums of different lengths and weights, and invented a device called a *pulsilogia*, which doctors could use for timing the pulse of a patient.

Most of the story is not true. The detailed experiments were carried out later, in 1602, and the *pulsilogia* was subsequently invented by a friend of Galileo's, using his discovery. But late in life Galileo told the story of watching the swinging chandelier to Vincenzo Viviani, who became Galileo's scribe after the great man went blind. Viviani wrote the first biography of Galileo, which always shows its subject in a good light, but is not always entirely accurate.

Although Galileo struggled to make a living, he did establish a reputation as a natural philosopher and began to carry out experiments and write down his ideas about the nature of the world, although he did not publish them at this time. In order to make progress in an academic career in those days, it was essential to have an influential patron. Galileo found one in the form of the Marquis Guidobaldo del Monte, an aristocrat with a keen interest in science (and he was no dilettante – he had written an important book on mechanics). Partly thanks to del Monte's influence, in 1589 Galileo became Professor of Mathematics at the University of Pisa – the same university he had left, without a degree, just four years earlier.

Mathematics was not regarded as a very important discipline, and the salary associated with this position was low compared with what other professors earned: a mere 60 crowns a year, compared with the 2,000 crowns received by the Professor of Medicine. But it was a start. Galileo augmented his income by private tuition – not just giving the benefit of his knowledge to students for the odd hour at a time, but taking in lodgers, the sons of the rich and powerful, who lived in his house and received the benefit of contact with the teacher at all hours. This was a standard procedure. But for Galileo it not only helped him to make ends meet, but spread his fame as a teacher and thinker as the young men eventually finished their courses and returned home, some of them to other countries.

Galileo may have been a popular teacher, but he did not get on with the establishment at Pisa. He led a curious double life, diligently teaching the Aristotelian texts that were the backbone of his official courses at Pisa, but questioning the Aristotelian way of thinking more and more in private, and not always keeping such doubts to himself. He discussed these ideas with his students, argued with other professors, and wrote the first draft of a book, *On Motion*. At the last minute he decided not to publish the book – probably a wise decision, since this draft was a mixture of Aristotelianism and Galileo's own ideas, unlike the polished book published under the same title several years later.

The most famous story about Galileo's time at Pisa is another of those legends that may or may not be true, the story that he dropped cannonballs of different weights from the Leaning Tower to show his students that they reached the ground together. Once again, the source of the story is Vincenzo Viviani, who was only 17 when he began working for Galileo, and clearly hero-worshipped the old man. Like other stories in Viviani's biography it is based on Galileo's reminiscences, when Galileo himself was in his seventies.

At the very least, the dates may have got confused. The most compelling evidence against the story being true is that Galileo was never reluctant to blow his own trumpet,

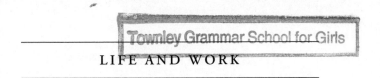

and he makes no mention of the demon-stration in any of his writings. But the idea was certainly in the air at the time. In 1586, a Flemish engineer, Simon Stevin, had carried out experiments in which he dropped lead weights from a height of about 10 metres, and had published his results.

What we do know is that there is a definite connection between Galileo, falling bodies and the Leaning Tower from three decades later, in 1612. That year, one of the Peripa-tetic professors at Pisa who wanted to show that Galileo's ideas about motion were wrong dropped objects of different weights from the Tower, and gleefully pointed out that they failed to hit the ground at *exactly* the same time. Galileo's response was typical of the man:

> Aristotle says that a hundred-pound ball falling from a height of a hundred cubits hits the ground before a one-pound ball has fallen one cubit. I say they arrive at the same time. You find, on making the test, that the larger ball beats the smaller one by two inches. Now, behind those two inches you want to hide Aristotle's ninety-nine

cubits and, speaking only of my tiny error, remain silent about his enormous mistake.

Along with his scientific free-thinking, Galileo, still only in his twenties, openly scoffed at the pomposity of the professors at Pisa, ridiculing their official uniform of the toga. He enjoyed life, including, literally, wine, women and song, plus good food; many surviving letters to or from distant friends over the course of his life mention the gift of a barrel of wine. Well before his three-year appointment came to an end, it became clear that Galileo didn't really fit in at the university, and that the appointment would not be renewed. In any case, Galileo had his eyes set on higher things, and began campaigning, with the aid of his patrons, to capture the more prestigious and better-paid Chair of Mathematics at the University of Padua.

The need to boost his income became more urgent when his father died in 1591, making Galileo the head of the family, and burdening him with heavy debts. Before he died, Vincenzio had promised a substantial dowry to his daughter Virginia, for which Galileo and his brother Michelangelo now found themselves responsible. Unfortunately, far from paying his share, Michelangelo, who later became a musician, would frequently come to Galileo for financial support for the rest of his own life.

Padua was part of the Venetian Republic, a rich and powerful state that had one of the most enlightened governments in Italy, tolerating all kinds of ideas that were frowned upon in Rome. In order to press his claims to the Chair of Mathematics in Padua (about 30 kilometres from Venice), Galileo travelled to Venice, where he was helped by the Tuscan Ambassador. He put on an impressive display of his ability and charm, making influential new friends, including Gianvincenzio Pinelli (a wealthy intellectual who owned a large library of books and manuscripts), and finding a new patron in the form of General Francesco del Monte (the younger brother of Guidobaldo). He managed to secure the position for four years (at a salary of 180 crowns a year), with an option for the head of the republic, the Doge, to renew it for a further two years if he wished. All Galileo now needed was the permission of the Grand Duke of Tuscany, Ferdinando, to take up this appointment with a foreign state. It seems to have been granted without a second thought, and Galileo started his new job in October 1592. He was 28 years old, and was to spend 18 years as Professor of Mathematics in Padua. He later said that these were the happiest years of his life.

The liberal-minded intellectual community of Padua extended beyond the university, and one focus of its activity was the house of Galileo's new friend, Pinelli, where he stayed until he could find a suitable house of his own. There, he was able to use Pinelli's large library, and he met people who would figure strongly in his life in later years, including Paolo Sarpi and Robert Bellarmine.

In public life, Galileo made his name with a treatise on military fortifications. This was a subject of keen interest and considerable importance to the Venetian state, which maintained its position of strength as much through military power as through trade. There quickly followed a book on mechanics, based on the lectures he was giving in Padua. Bizarrely, to modern eyes, in those days it was still widely believed – and taught – that a large weight could be lifted by a small force, with no trade-off. As Galileo's book developed through several editions, he began to spell out clearly that this was not possible, that you can't get something for nothing.

In systems consisting of levers or pulleys what is really happening, he explained, is that a small force moving through a large distance is shifting a large weight through a small distance. In a neat analogy, he explained that it was as if the large weight were divided up into a set of smaller weights, which were shifted in turn by the small force. So, for example, in a pulley system where a 1-kilogram weight lifts a 10-kilogram weight through 1 metre, the 1-kilogram weight moves down through 10 metres, just as if it had made 10 journeys, each of 1 metre, to lift 10 single 1-kilogram weights through 1 metre each.

Money was constantly a problem to Galileo during his time in Padua, and he was continually striving to come up with an invention that would make him rich – rich enough, at least, to meet his obligations to his family. One of his inventions, from around 1593, was an early kind of thermometer, a glass tube with a bulbous swelling in one end, and open at the other end. The tube was heated to expel air, and then placed upright in a bowl of

water, with the open end under the water.
Water rose up the tube as the remaining air
in it cooled and contracted. Then, like an
upside-down version of the modern thermometer, when it was warmer the air in the bulb
would expand, pushing the water level down-
ward. It was ingenious, but not very practical
(not least because the water level in the tube
depended on air pressure, as well as tempera-
ture) and it made no money. Another invention – successful technically but never
commercially – was a system for lifting water
for irrigation.

In 1595 or 1596, though, Galileo came up
with a modest winner. Known as a 'compass',
it was actually a kind of all-purpose calculating instrument, a forerunner of the slide rule
– an essential scientific implement in the days
before pocket calculators. Galileo's compass
started life as a device for gunners to use in
calculating elevations when ranging their
guns. It was a distinct improvement over the
existing procedure, which required the gun-
ner to stand in front of the gun and hang a
device rather like a carpenter's set square in
its mouth – not the safest place to be in the
heat of battle. (Incidentally, the elevations on

this older form of gauge were marked off in intervals of 7.5 degrees of arc, called 'points'. The lowest point, for zero elevation, was blank, so the term 'point blank' came to refer to very short range gunnery.)

By 1597 Galileo had adapted his gunnery aid to include scales showing the relative densities of various metals, lines for calculating cube roots and square roots, and other data useful in geometrical applications. The instrument was such a success that for a brief period he had to employ a skilled artisan to make them; but he sold them relatively cheaply, and made his money out of the idea from the tuition fees he charged for teaching purchasers how to use them.

It was just as well that Galileo found a temporary new source of income when he did, because at the end of the 1590s and into the beginning of the seventeenth century his financial commitments increased. First, he formed an alliance with a local woman, Marina Gamba. They never married (indeed, they never lived under the same roof), but formed a stable relationship which lasted more than ten years, and which produced three children: daughters in 1600 and 1601, and a son in 1606. Marina was a commoner, and such liaisons were themselves common in Italy in those days, but kept fairly discreet. Although the couple were clearly more than fond of each other, the status of their relationship was made quite clear when Galileo made his servants godparents to the children. Nevertheless, he loved the children dearly, and his son, Vincenzio, was later legitimized and became his heir.

In 1601, Galileo's younger sister, Livia, married, and together with Michelangelo he promised a substantial dowry. Michelangelo never paid his share. He tried his luck as a musician, first in Poland and then in Germany, each time with the aid of money 'borrowed' from Galileo but never repaid. Galileo kept himself afloat financially by taking in students, as he always had, getting advances against his salary, and borrowing money in his turn from rich friends. Notable among these was Giovanfrancesco Sagredo, a wealthy nobleman nine years younger than Galileo, a bachelor who could easily afford to help his friend out.

Galileo did not let his financial difficulties stop him from enjoying a full and happy life.

He visited Venice regularly, and often went on trips into the hills near Padua, staying in the villas of his friends. One of these trips (probably in 1603) had unfortunate long-term consequences. On a hot day, after some healthy walking and a hearty meal, Galileo and his companions went to sleep in a room equipped with a kind of air conditioning, connected by ducts to cool caves. The ventilators leading to the caves were closed when the party went to sleep, but were then opened by a servant. Galileo and his two companions became severely ill as a result – so ill that one of them died. Something more than just the effects of cold, damp air on hot, overfed bodies must have been involved; perhaps toxic gases from the caves entered the room along with the cool air. For the rest of his life Galileo suffered repeated bouts of illness, which he blamed on this incident. Attacks would leave him confined to his bed for weeks at a time with arthritic pains.

But none of this seriously affected his scientific work. It was in Padua that he carried out detailed experiments with pendulums, and studied acceleration by timing the motion of balls rolling down inclined planes – although very little of this would be made public until the 1630s. Always, Galileo carried out experiments for himself to test hypotheses and find out how nature worked, rejecting the abstract 'philosophical' approach of the Peripatetics. He investigated the power of magnets, and made the acquaintance (through correspondence) of Johannes Kepler, an enthusiastic supporter of the Copernican idea that the Earth moves around the Sun. It was in a letter to Kepler written in May 1597 that Galileo first expressed in writing his own support for the Copernican cosmology.

Alongside all this, Galileo studied literature and poetry, played the lute for pleasure, attended the theatre, and enjoyed evenings out drinking with his friends. He was 40 in 1604, and could look back on a decade in which he had lived life to the full, established a reputation for the practical application of science of immense value to the Venetian State, become a popular lecturer, and begun to gain a reputation as an anti-Aristotelian – something which, if anything, only enhanced his reputation in free-thinking Venice and Padua. The student 'wrangler' was now a man well able to argue a case, often using biting wit and sarcasm (as well as impeccable scientific arguments) to demolish an opponent's case. His post at the University of Padua had not only been renewed, but with a salary increase. All in all, life was pretty good for the 40-year-old Galileo.

It was also in 1604 that Galileo first emerged as an astronomer. This was the result of the appearance in the sky of a 'new' star, or nova, in October that year – a star so bright that today it would be called a supernova. We now know that a supernova is an old, dim star that suddenly flares into unusual brightness in one last burst of explosive activity at the end of its life.

According to Aristotle, the celestial sphere beyond the Moon was perfect and unchanging. So any new heavenly phenomena, such as novas or comets, must exist in the region between the Earth and the Moon. Galileo studied the new star carefully, using surveying techniques (he was, after all, an expert military surveyor) to see if it showed any sign of movement relative to the other stars, but there was none. In a series of widely acclaimed public lectures, he argued that this object was indeed at a distance typical of the known stars, and that therefore, contrary to Aristotelian doctrine, the celestial sphere was not perfect and unchanging. This led to a fierce debate with the Professor of Philosophy at Padua, Cesare Cremonini, who defended the Aristotelian position (fierce, but amicable; there was no personal animosity between Cremonini and Galileo, who remained friends). All of this added to Galileo's growing reputation, and helped to convince him of the superiority of the experimental method over abstract philosophy.

During the summer of 1605 Galileo visited Florence, where he had pressing business to attend to. Both his brothers-in-law were suing him for non-payment of the instalments on the dowries of his sisters. He was being kept afloat only by his friend Sagredo, who had paid court fees and was stalling the Florentine legal process as best he could. In spite of his professional success and happy position at Padua, Galileo had always wanted to return to Tuscany, and in particular to get a court appointment, which would free him from the time-consuming obligation to give lectures. Now, he was presented with a golden opportunity to promote his cause – the Grand

Duchess, Christina, asked Galileo to give her son Cosimo tuition in the use of his military compass. With Galileo seen to be in favour at court, the litigation against him faded away. Perhaps Christina expressed her disapproval, or perhaps the litigants now reckoned that the money owed them would soon be forthcoming if Galileo's star remained in the ascendant.

Until now, Galileo had only circulated manuscript copies of his instructions on the use of the compass, mainly because he wanted to restrict knowledge of its use as much as possible, so that he could still charge tuition fees for explaining it. But in 1606 he published the manual as a printed book, in a strictly limited edition of 60 copies, dedicated to Prince Cosimo.

While Galileo continued to make overtures to the Tuscan Court, a political dispute flared up between Venice and Rome. A new Pope, Paul V, had been elected in 1605, and he was now attempting to exert the authority of the Vatican in matters of taxation, border disputes and the sovereignty of the Doge of Venice. Matters escalated to the point where, on 17 April 1606, the Doge was excommunicated. The Jesuits were expelled from Venice, and war seemed inevitable; but eventually the crisis passed, and Venice retained its large measure of independence from Rome.

During this crisis, a leading figure on the Venetian side was Friar Paolo Sarpi. Twelve years older than Galileo, Sarpi had befriended him on his arrival at Padua, and Galileo looked up to the friar as 'my father and my master'. Sarpi incurred the hatred of the Jesuits, as did anyone associated with him. In October 1607, an assassination attempt left Sarpi desperately wounded, but he recovered; the would-be assassins escaped to Rome, where they were well treated by the Pope.

With all this going on around him, and his campaign for a post in Tuscany gaining pace with the ascent of Prince Cosimo to the throne (as Grand Duke Cosimo II), Galileo continued to develop his masterwork – a book on mechanics, inertia and motion. He also studied magnetism, hydrostatics, and the strength of different materials. It was at about this time that he realized, and proved, that the path of a projectile fired from a gun, or thrown through the air, is a parabola. It was still widely believed that if, for example, a cannon fired a ball horizontally, the ball would travel a certain distance in a straight line, and then fall straight down to the ground, rather than following a curved trajectory. Even those thinkers who had noticed that the actual trajectory followed by a cannonball was a curve did not know what *kind* of curve it was.

In 1609, Galileo was in his pomp. A leading figure in the Venetian state, he was 45 years old, secure in his post, still with financial worries, but working to complete what he knew would be a great book. Even if the views expressed in that book displeased the Pope, he would be safe to express them as long as he stayed where he was. But he still hankered after the freedom that an appointment as Court Mathematician in Tuscany would bring him – freedom from lecturing, financial security, and a return to the hills that he loved. In the summer of 1609, the opportunity to fulfil all those dreams fell into his lap.

The telescope had been invented by Hans Lippershey, in Holland, the previous year (probably re-invented; it has quite recently been shown that Leonard Digges, in England, almost certainly built telescopes before 1550).

News of the invention spread quickly across Europe, and Paolo Sarpi heard of it in a letter from one of Galileo's former pupils, a French nobleman then living in Paris, before the end of 1608. It isn't clear whether the news didn't reach Galileo at that time, or whether he dismissed the story as fiction; perhaps Sarpi didn't take much notice and failed to pass the news on. But in July 1609 Galileo visited Venice, where he discussed the invention with Sarpi, and was shown the letter in which the telescope was described. We can imagine the dollar signs scrolling through his eyes like a cartoon character with a get-rich-quick scheme. An instrument which could make distant objects visible would be of enormous value to a maritime power such as Venice.

While Galileo was in Venice, news came at the beginning of August that a stranger, a Dutchman, had arrived in Padua with one of the miraculous instruments. Galileo rushed home to find out more, only to discover that the stranger had already departed for Venice, where he intended to sell the telescope to the Doge. Aghast, and with very little to go on, Galileo began a frantic burst of experimentation, trying out lenses in tubes to make his own telescope. The design that he hit upon used one convex lens and one concave; unlike the Dutch version, which featured two convex lenses, this happens to give an upright image of the object being viewed. Within 24 hours, Galileo had a working telescope. On 4 August, a pre-arranged message was despatched to Sarpi, who had just been asked by the Venetian Senate for advice about the telescope now being offered to them by the itinerant Dutchman.

Sarpi effectively froze the Dutchman out of the picture, giving Galileo time to build a beautiful instrument, with a magnifying power of 10, in a tooled leather case. Galileo arrived back in Venice before the end of the month, and demonstrated his instrument to sensational effect, among other things giving the senators a clear view of galleys far out to sea, two hours before they became visible to the naked eye. In a final gesture of genius, showing his political nous, Galileo presented the telescope to the Doge as a free gift. In return, he was offered tenure in his post in Padua for life, at double his present salary, giving him 1,000 crowns a year.

Galileo accepted, but then discovered the

snags. The increased salary was not to be paid until the following year, and tenure for life also meant teaching for life. A quick visit to Florence gave him an opportunity to demonstrate the telescope to Cosimo II, and by December 1609 Galileo had constructed a telescope with a magnifying power of 20. It was this instrument that he turned to the heavens and used to discover the four brightest moons of Jupiter early in 1610. He named them the 'Medicean stars', in a further attempt to curry favour in Florence. With his powerful new telescope (about as powerful as a decent pair of modern binoculars), Galileo looked at the Milky Way, and found that it was made up of a myriad of individual stars. He looked at the Moon, and found that instead of being a perfectly smooth sphere it was pockmarked with craters and had mountains which he measured, from the length of their shadows, to be 6 kilometres high (a slight overestimate compared with modern measurements). In March 1610, these amazing discoveries were published in his book *The Starry Messenger*, dedicated (of course) to Grand Duke Cosimo II de' Medici.

The book was such an extraordinary suc-

cess that Galileo got only six copies of the
first printing of 550. It has been described as
the most important book of the seventeenth
century, and only five years after its publication it had been translated into Chinese and
published in China. The whole literate world
knew of Galileo and his discoveries. The book
was also a success in assisting Galileo's campaign in Florence. Having decided that,
because he had not yet started receiving the
promised increase in salary, he had no obligations in Venice or Padua, he campaigned
shamelessly for a post in Tuscany. In May
1610 his efforts were rewarded. He was to
become Chief Mathematician of the University of Pisa and Philosopher and Mathematician to the Grand Duke for life, with a salary
of 1,000 crowns a year. He would have no
teaching duties whatsoever, and the Grand
Duke released him from the legal obligation
to cover Michelangelo's remaining unpaid
share of the two dowries, on which Galileo
had more than covered his own original obligations. He was to take up the post in
October.

The turmoil of the move and its implica-
tions completely altered Galileo's private life,

as well as his professional prospects. His two daughters moved to Florence just before he did, initially staying with his mother; his son stayed in Padua with Marina Gamba until he was old enough to join Galileo. But Marina stayed in Padua, seemingly as a result of an entirely amicable split. The passion had died, and she didn't want to move, while Galileo didn't much mind leaving her behind. In Florence, Galileo soon made the friendship of a young nobleman in the mould of Sagredo – Filippo Salviati, 20 years younger than Galileo, who was wealthy, interested in science, and loved fine wine and good food. There could be no doubt that Galileo had fallen on his feet, although his pleasure was temporarily dampened by one of his recurring bouts of ill-health early in 1611.

Before Galileo left Padua, he discovered that there was something strange about the appearance of Saturn; only after Galileo's death was this strange appearance explained, by Christiaan Huygens, as being due to a system of rings around the planet. Soon after he arrived in Florence, he discovered the phases of Venus, in which the appearance of the planet changes in the same way that the appearance of the Moon changes as it orbits the Earth. This was a killer-blow to the Aristotelian cosmology, since the only explanation for the phases is that Venus orbits the Sun.

The desperation with which the Peripatetics tried to explain the new discoveries is highlighted by one bizarre suggestion, made by one of the philosophers in Florence. He said that the mountains and craters Galileo had observed on the Moon were real, but that all of these surface irregularities were encased in an invisible sphere of perfectly smooth, perfectly transparent crystal! Galileo retorted that he would be happy to accept this possibility, provided he was allowed to claim that there were mountains of this crystal ten times higher than any mountains he had actually observed on the Moon.

Around this time, Galileo also observed sunspots, unaware that these had already been seen by other astronomers with the aid of telescopes. Like all the previous telescopic discoveries, this too flew in the face of Aristotelianism, and it was important to find out how the Church would react to the news. Once safely settled in Florence, there was one place Galileo just had to go to spread the word – Rome.

Unlike Venice, Tuscany was very much part of the politics of Rome, and the Medicis had numbered cardinals and popes among their ranks. To put things in a broader perspective, this period was at the height of the Counter-Reformation: the period, roughly a hundred years long, in which the Catholic Church conducted a vigorous campaign against Protestantism. You might think that this would be a bad time to question the Aristotelian tradition which the Church had made its own. But in the spring of 1611, Galileo was fêted almost as much in Rome as he had been in Venice and Florence. He was careful not to proclaim the death of Aristotelianism, preferring to let the evidence speak for itself as he showed influential people, including cardinals, the wonders to be seen with the aid of a telescope. The Pope granted him an audience, and he was made a member of what is reckoned to be the first scientific society in the world, the Lincean Academy ('Academy of Lynxes'), founded in 1603. Largely thanks to Galileo's influence, this talking-shop soon became an important body, the first independent group of scientific thinkers, unattached to any university and owing allegiance to no one. It was, incidentally, at one of the society's dinners held during Galileo's visit that the term 'telescope' was coined.

Among the old friends Galileo met in Rome was Robert Bellarmine, now a cardinal (and member of the Inquisition) himself. As the records show, one small cloud appeared on the horizon at the time of this visit. Probably because Galileo did cautiously mention to Bellarmine that his astronomical observations could be seen as supporting the Copernican cosmology, with the Earth moving around the Sun, Bellarmine wrote to the Inquisition in Venice to check whether Galileo had ever been formally implicated in teaching Copernican ideas. But there the matter rested – for the time being.

Back in Florence, Galileo continued his astronomical observations. He was particularly keen to find a way to use the changing positions of Jupiter's satellites as a kind of cosmic clock, so that navigators might determine the time accurately and therefore calculate their longitude, the key problem in navigation in the seventeenth century. He also studied hydrostatics, and wrote a little book on the subject which sold out twice in 1612. Even before his visit to Rome, he had begun to use the magnifying power of lenses as a form of microscope, magnifying the parts of insects to the wonder of his acquaintances. But his most important activity at this time was the study of sunspots.

Galileo wrote a book on sunspots, published by the Lincean Academy in 1613. In a flowery preface, the Linceans asserted that Galileo had discovered sunspots. This led to a bitter row with a German Jesuit, Christopher Scheiner, who also claimed priority for the discovery. (Ironically, the telescopic observations of sunspots had already been carried out, and published, before either of them got in on the act, by the Dutchman Johann Fabricius, so the argument was pointless.) Scheiner claimed that sunspots were tiny planets, orbiting close to the Sun; Galileo proved that they were blemishes on the face of the Sun, and that their motion was caused by the Sun's rotation. In other words, the Sun itself was imperfect.

This argument made another bitter enemy for Galileo in the Jesuit camp, but the work on sunspots is especially interesting for another reason. It was in an appendix to the sunspot book that, for the first and only time in print, Galileo came out unambiguously as a supporter of Copernican cosmology, citing the evidence of the movement of the 'Medicean stars' around Jupiter and the way these moons are regularly eclipsed.

Although otherwise still extremely cautious about what he put down in print, Galileo began to speak out more openly in support of Copernican ideas, and to argue that the Bible should not be regarded always as the literal truth, but sometimes as metaphor. Complaints were made, in a general sort of way, to the Inquisition in Rome, but without any specific charges being laid against Galileo. No action was taken, and at the end of 1615 Galileo voluntarily visited Rome (with the official permission of his Grand Duke, and staying in the Tuscan Ambassador's residence while in Rome) to find out exactly where he stood, and to argue the case for the new astronomy if the officials there would listen. This was a serious misjudgment, and brought matters to a head in an unfortunate fashion.

The expert theologians deliberated on the

two key issues, and responded with an opinion backed by the full weight of Catholic doctrine. It was officially decreed that the idea that the Sun lies at the centre of the Universe was 'foolish and absurd . . . and formally heretical', while the idea that the Earth moves through space was decreed to be 'at the very least erroneous in faith'.

On 24 February 1616, the Pope instructed Cardinal Bellarmine (who was known to be sympathetic to Galileo) to notify Galileo of the decision. The Pope's instructions were quite specific – Bellarmine was to tell Galileo that he could not 'hold or defend' either of the notions that had been pronounced upon. If, and only if, Galileo objected to this, he was to be warned formally by the Inquisition, in the presence of a notary and witnesses, that he must not 'hold, defend *or teach*' (our italics) these Copernican ideas. The distinction was crucial. If he were allowed to teach Copernicanism, Galileo could use it as an example of what other people thought, even if he did not (at least, not officially) hold those views himself. At this point, events become cloudy.

There seems to have been a single meeting

between Galileo and Bellarmine, with the representatives of the Inquisition, notary and witnesses all present. In what seems to be an official (but unsigned) record of that meeting, Bellarmine is stated to have issued the first set of instructions to Galileo, then immediately, leaving no time for Galileo to react, the other representatives of the Inquisition issued the second warning, including the crucial reference to teaching.

The historian Stillman Drake has reconstructed the probable course of events. He argues persuasively that the deposition remained unsigned because Bellarmine (the senior official present, and the direct representative of the Pope in this matter) was furious that the Pope's explicit instructions had not been obeyed, and regarded only his initial warning to Galileo (who had not objected) as having any legal standing. Indeed, when rumours began to spread that Galileo had been punished in some way by the Inquisition, Bellarmine supplied him with a formal affidavit stating that this was not so: Galileo had merely been informed of the general edict, which applied to all Catholics equally. The two documents – the unsigned 'minutes' of the meeting and Bellarmine's signed affidavit – were to prove crucial in Galileo's eventual trial for heresy.

The trial is the climax to Galileo's life-story, and is what we are now rushing towards. We shall say little more about Galileo's other work – his continuing studies of the moons of Jupiter, his investigations of comets, the slow progress with his great book. But we cannot move on without mentioning one strange aspect of his private life.

In the spring of 1617, Galileo moved into a fine house known as Bellosguardo, on a hill to the west of Florence. The main reason for the move was that he wanted to be near his daughters, Virginia and Livia, who were entering the order of the Poor Clares, in a convent in nearby Arcetri. They had no choice – Galileo seems to have been determined that his daughters would spend their lives as nuns. From a practical point of view, after his bad experiences with the dowries of his sisters, we can see why he was eager to ensure that he would neither have to support his daughters as unmarriageable illegitimate children, nor pay a substantial dowry to get them off his hands.

The fact that he could do this even though he loved them dearly enough to move to be near them looks odd to modern eyes, especially since the Poor Clares really were poor, and he was committing the girls, at the age of 16, to a life of hard work, cold accommodation and inadequate food. But that is what he did, and in spite of everything remained particularly close to the older girl, who took the name Maria Celeste; her sister became known as Arcangela.

In 1617, Galileo was 53 years old. As well as his long-standing illness, he now suffered from a severe hernia. He had achieved fame and (relative) fortune, and had been warned off by the Pope, if only in a gentle sort of way, from getting too closely associated with Copernicanism. A year later, the Thirty Years' War (a Catholic–Protestant clash) began, and common sense would have ordained that he avoid annoying the Church further. But in 1618, three comets were seen, and this led Galileo back into public debate with the Jesuits, in the person of Orazio Grassi.

Grassi published a book about comets, to which Galileo replied in withering terms. We won't go into details, since both the Jesuits and Galileo were wrong, on this occasion, in their explanations of the phenomenon. But in his book *The Assayer*, published in 1623, Galileo also summed up his understanding of the scientific method. Sarcastically suggesting that his opponents seemed to think that 'philosophy is a book of fiction by some author, like *The Iliad*', he said that the book of the Universe:

> cannot be understood unless one first learns to comprehend the language and to understand the alphabet in which it is composed. It is written in the language of mathematics, and its characters are triangles, circles and other geometric figures, without which it is humanly impossible to understand a single word of it; without these, one wanders about in a dark labyrinth.

In other words, the Jesuits were dealing in fairy tales, while Galileo was dealing in facts.

Just as *The Assayer* was about to be published, the Pope died (this was Gregory XV, who had succeeded Paul V in 1621), and was replaced by Maffeo Barberini, who took the name Urban VIII. This seemed to be a stroke of luck for Galileo. The two had been on friendly terms when Barberini was a Cardinal, and even better Galileo had tutored one of Barberini's nephews, Francesco, who received his doctorate in Pisa a few months before Urban VIII was elected. In a fine example of nepotism, Francesco Barberini became a Cardinal himself almost as soon as his uncle was made Pope – another friend for Galileo in the Vatican.

The change of Pope seemed more than sufficient compensation for the death of the Grand Duke of Tuscany, Cosimo II, in 1621. Cosimo had been succeeded by the 11-year old Ferdinando II, with his mother Christina as regent, seriously weakening the voice of Tuscany in Italian politics, and therefore weakening Galileo's own political power base. In 1623, there was just time to ensure that the printed version of *The Assayer* was dedicated to the new Pope, and Galileo was delighted to hear that Urban VIII had enjoyed it so much that he had had extracts read aloud to him while he was dining.

In April 1624, Galileo visited Rome to pay

his respects to the new Pope, and to Cardinal Barberini. He stayed until June, and was granted six audiences with the Pope, who gave him a gold medal and other honours, and wrote on his departure to the young Duke Ferdinando II, praising Galileo and his science. Galileo left under the clear impression that he had permission to publish his long-planned book comparing the Copernican and the Aristotelian world-views, provided he only argued the Copernican case hypothetically, and did not claim that science proved that the Earth moved.

In Galileo's own mind, of course, the case *was* proven. Ironically, though, what he regarded as his best evidence was completely mistaken. Perhaps naturally for an inhabitant of the Mediterranean region, Galileo likened the tides to the motion of water sloshing to and fro in a tub when the tub was moved. He was so sure that the tides proved the motion of the Earth that he planned to call his book *Dialogue on the Tides*. He was dissuaded from doing so by friends, who suggested that the evidence provided by the tides in support of Copernicus was so strong that the mere mention of the word in the title of the book would be sure to attract the wrath of the Church.

A much more important feature of Galileo's work, to modern eyes, was his discovery of the idea of inertia. By rolling balls down an inclined plane and allowing them to roll up another plane, he came to see that in the absence of friction a ball would always roll up to the same height from which it had rolled down. (That throwaway phrase 'in the absence of friction' conceals another great leap made by Galileo, who – as is also apparent from his experiments with balls dropped from the Leaning Tower – was the first scientist to grasp and understand the idea of extrapolating from our imperfect experiments to some idealized world of pure science.) If the second plane was made more shallow, the ball would roll further, until it got back to its original height. And if the second plane was actually horizontal, and friction could be ignored, the ball could never regain its lost height, and so it would roll on for ever.

Galileo realized that motion was a natural state of things. His one mistake was that, because he knew the surface of the Earth to be round, so that horizontal motion (motion towards the horizon) means following part of the curved surface of the Earth, he thought that this natural inertial motion must follow a circle. This neatly explained, it seemed to him, why the planets orbited the Sun continually without being pushed.

Over the next few years, Galileo worked only intermittently on the book, plagued by ill-health, sometimes putting it to one side when the political climate seemed to shift against free thinking, sometimes getting sidetracked by other work. He also had to fight a tedious legal battle with the University of Pisa, which attempted to get out of the legal obligation imposed on them by Cosimo II to pay Galileo for doing nothing, even when he didn't live in Pisa. We can sympathize with the University, although this is a dispute that surely would not have arisen if the new Duke had been an adult. Eventually, Galileo won the case. And, under repeated prodding by his friends (who must have begun to wonder if he would die without completing it), the book did progress. By the beginning of 1630 it was completed, and needed only the approval of the censors in Rome before it could be published.

Now, things began to get complicated. We'll smooth over the complications as much as possible, but the key thing to understand is the way Galileo's book, *Dialogue Concerning the Two Chief Systems of the World*, was constructed. As the title suggests, it was in the form of a conversation between two people, one supporting each of the two opposing world-views. This was an old device, going back to the Ancient Greeks. Galileo added a third 'voice' in the book, a supposedly independent observer who listened in on the conversation and raised points for debate. The character who presented Galileo's views (arguing the Copernican case) was called Filippo Salviati, after Galileo's old friend, who had died in 1614. The independent observer was named Giovanfrancesco Sagredo, after his other friend, who had died in 1620. The supporter of Aristotle (or rather, strictly speaking, of the Earth-centred cosmology of Ptolemy) was called Simplicio, after an Ancient Greek who had written a commentary on Aristotle's work. It could be argued (tongue firmly in cheek) that this was an innocuous choice of a name borrowed from a genuine supporter of Aristotle. But Galileo undoubtedly intended to imply that anyone who supported Aristotle was a simpleton, and 'Simplicio' was to be a major factor in getting him in to hot episcopal water.

The book slowly made progress towards publication, with the censor demanding minor changes but taking no exception to the general tone of the book. A preface was required, spelling out the hypothetical nature of the ideas discussed, and some words had to be added at the end, making it clear that Aristotle was the approved choice of the Church. The point the Church wanted to get across in allowing the book to be published was that they were not scientific ignoramuses, lagging behind the rest of Europe. They were well aware of the scientific debate, and had made their decision on religious grounds, which brooked no argument – scientific or otherwise.

Originally, the book was to have been published in Rome by the Linceans, but the death of Prince Frederico Cesi, the Chief Lynx, threw the affairs of the Academy into turmoil, and permission was obtained to transfer the printing to Florence. An outbreak of plague made travel between Florence and Rome difficult, and delayed matters further. Printing began at last in June 1631, and the finished copies of the book (an edition of a thousand copies) went on sale in Florence in March 1632, with some copies being sent to Rome as fast as the plague permitted.

Cardinal Barberini wrote to Galileo expressing his delight with the book, but others were less pleased. Galileo's old Jesuit enemies were angered by, among other things, the repetition in the *Dialogue* of his claim to have discovered sunspots first. Somebody noticed that the preface required by the censor had been set in a different typeface from the rest of the book, effectively distancing Galileo from it. And the Pope's own words, stating the truth of the Aristotelian worldview, had been placed in the mouth of Simplicio. Could it be that Galileo was saying that the Pope was a fool?

In fairness, since Simplicio is the only character in the book who supported Aristotle, the words insisted on by the censor could hardly have been spoken by either of the other characters. But the choice of name, which must have seemed such a great joke to Galileo when he started writing the book, turned out not to have been a good move. And then, with the ground prepared by all this having been pointed out to the Pope, some unknown person with a grudge against Galileo dug out of the files the unsigned minute from 1616, forbidding Galileo to 'hold, defend *or teach*' the Copernican world-view. On the evidence he had before him, it seemed to Urban VIII that Galileo had deliberately flouted the orders of one of his papal predecessors.

All of this roused Urban VIII to a fury. Galileo was summoned to Rome to stand trial for heresy – for writing a book which had been passed by the official censor! Pleading old age and (genuine) infirmity, he postponed the evil moment as long as possible, but on 13 April 1633, when Galileo was in his 70th year, the infamous trial began.

Galileo was totally unfazed. He trumped the production of the unsigned minute by producing the signed affidavit from Bellarmine (who had died in 1621), which required him only to refrain from holding or defending Copernican ideas, not from teaching them hypothetically. He claimed that since Paul V and Bellarmine had put him right in 1616, he had indeed stopped believing such nonsense, and taught it only out of scientific interest. By any conventional legal test, Galileo had won. His documentary evidence beat the prosecution's into a cocked hat, quite apart from the fact that his book literally had the official seal of approval. But nobody beat the Inquisition. Once the wheels were set in motion, somebody had to take the rap.

With Cardinal Barberini acting as intermediary, there followed a long process of what would now be called plea bargaining. Galileo understood that if he admitted wrong-doing, that in his enthusiasm to present sound arguments in his book he had gone too far, he would get a light sentence. He made the confession (after some heavy persuasion by Barberini, who knew only too well what might happen to his old friend), and was stunned when, on 22 June, the formal sentence of life imprisonment was read out to him at a ceremony in front of the assembled Cardinals of the Inquisition. Even then, three of the ten Cardinals (including Barberini) refused to sign the sentence; he went down only on a majority verdict.

It sounds harsh, but remember that in those days the maximum sentence he could have got was torture on the rack, followed by burning at the stake. In comparison, life imprisonment *is* a soft option. And it was Cardinal Barberini who ensured that the incarceration started out in the grounds of the Tuscan Embassy in Rome, then shifted to the custody of the Archbishop of Siena (another Galileo sympathizer) and ended up in Galileo's own home, now in Arcetri, as nothing more than house arrest, from the beginning of 1634. Sadly, on 2 April that year, his favourite daughter, Sister Maria Celeste, died.

In his enforced 'retirement', Galileo overcame his many disappointments. He turned back to his work, completing his greatest book, *Two New Sciences*, which was smuggled out of Italy in manuscript form and published in Leyden in 1638 by Louis Elzevir. This great book summed up all of Galileo's work, on mechanics, inertia, pendulums, the strength of bodies and the scientific method. It was of enormous influence in the decades that followed – and, like all Galileo's works, assured of an enthusiastic readership throughout Protestant Europe precisely because of

Galileo's conflict with the Catholic establish-ment. It is no coincidence that after the 1630s Italian science went into decline, while dra-matic new developments occurred to the north and west, especially in Britain. Among Galileo's visitors in his final years were Thomas Hobbes, who brought news of an English translation of the *Dialogue*, and John Milton, on a tour of Europe at the age of 29.

By the time *Two New Sciences* appeared in print, Galileo had gone blind. Even after losing his sight, he invented an escapement for a pendulum clock, which he described to his son Vincenzio; the clock was built after Galileo died. (The spread of similar clocks across Europe followed the independent work of Christiaan Huygens.) In Galileo's last years, from late in 1638, Vincenzo Viviani joined him as his scribe and assistant, and would eventually write the first biography of the great man. Galileo remained mentally active to the end, though growing physically more frail, and died peacefully in his sleep, on the night of 8/9 January 1642, a few weeks short of his 78th birthday.

There is no evidence that he ever uttered the words *eppur, si muove* ('yet it does move') as he was led from the Inquisition after formal sentence was passed. If he had, he surely would not have lived for the best part of a further nine years.

# Afterword

It is impossible to overstate the importance of Galileo in establishing the scientific method of investigating the world. His specific scientific achievements were impressive enough. He built with his own hands the telescopes (the best of his day) he used to study the skies, and through those observations he found compelling evidence that the Earth is not at the centre of the Universe. He was the first person to appreciate the role of forces in determining the way things move. To the Peripatetics, some things just had a natural tendency to rise, and others a natural tendency to fall, but Galileo said that all motion except his version of inertial motion must be due to a force.

The idea of inertia that he introduced was not quite right, but it was an impressive step forward from Aristotelian ideas. This idea was taken up by René Descartes, who realized that it actually applied to motion in a straight line, not to circular motion. From Descartes, the idea of inertia was picked up by Isaac Newton, and became the basis of his first law of motion. And since the real 'natural tendency' of an object such as a planet is to move in a straight line unless acted upon by an external force, that in turn was a key insight in developing the law of gravity, explaining why the planets are held in orbit around the Sun.

To put all this in perspective, as late as the 1620s the philosophers were still arguing about what would happen to a heavy object dropped from the top of the mast of a moving ship. Notice that they did not actually drop things from the masts of moving ships to find out what happened, they just argued the issue to arrive at the answer by pure reason. Some said that the object would be left behind by the motion of the ship; others that it would move forward with the motion of the ship and fall at the foot of the mast. Of course, the second idea is correct, as Galileo was careful to find out by talking to mariners. The falling object preserves the forward motion it started out with. The definitive version of this specific experiment was carried out as late as 1640, only two years before Galileo died, when the Frenchman Pierre Gassendi borrowed a galley from the French navy and dropped a series of balls from the mast to the deck below while it was being rowed flat out across the smooth Mediterranean. (A grim modern example of this conservation of momentum can be seen in any film footage of a 'stick' of bombs falling from an aircraft.)

Gassendi was strongly influenced by Galileo's writings, and this highlights the real revolution that Galileo brought to the study of the world. He established the idea of scientific experiments, and the whole business of testing hypotheses by getting your hands dirty investigating the real world, instead of strolling about discussing it in philosophical terms. This experimental approach was enthusiastically espoused by Isaac Newton, and well before the end of the seventeenth century it was installed as *the* scientific method. Everything else, from the law of gravity, to quantum physics, black holes and our understanding of the structure of DNA and the genetic code, followed from that beginning. As Stephen Hawking has put it:

Galileo, perhaps more than any other single person, was responsible for the birth of modern science . . . [he] was one of the first to argue that man could hope to understand how the world works, and, more-over, that we could do this by observing the real world.

Eventually, even the Catholic Church had to agree. In 1992, a commission under Cardinal Paul Poupard found that Galileo had been 'more perceptive' in his interpretation of the Bible than his prosecutors. Moreover, the commission conceded that, as Galileo had suggested, the Bible should be regarded as not always telling the literal truth, but sometimes as metaphor. The Pope, John Paul II, formally pardoned Galileo on 31 October 1992, some 350 years after he had died. *Eppur*, indeed, *si muove*.

# A brief history of science

*c.* 2000 BC    First phase of construction at Stonehenge, an early observatory.

430 BC    Democritus teaches that everything is made of atoms.

*c.* 330 BC    Aristotle teaches that the Universe is made of concentric spheres, centred on the Earth.

300 BC    Euclid gathers together and writes down the mathematical knowledge of his time.

265 BC    Archimedes discovers his principle of buoyancy while having a bath.

*c.* 235 BC    Eratosthenes of Cyrene calculates the size of the Earth with commendable accuracy.

AD 79 — Pliny the Elder dies while studying an eruption of Mount Vesuvius.

400 — The term 'chemistry' is used for the first time, by scholars in Alexandria.

c. 1020 — Alhazen, the greatest scientist of the so-called Dark Ages, explains the workings of lenses and parabolic mirrors.

1054 — Chinese astronomers observe a supernova; the remnant is visible today as the Crab Nebula.

1490 — Leonardo da Vinci studies the capillary action of liquids.

1543 — In his book *De revolutionibus*, Nicholas Copernicus places the Sun, not the Earth, at the centre of the Solar System. Andreas Vesalius studies human anatomy in a scientific way.

c. 1550 — The reflecting telescope, and

later the refracting telescope, pioneered by Leonard Digges.

1572    Tycho Brahe observes a supernova.

1580    Prospero Alpini realizes that plants come in two sexes.

1596    Botanical knowledge is summarized in John Gerrard's *Herbal*.

1608    Hans Lippershey's invention of a refracting telescope is the first for which there is firm evidence.

1609–19    Johannes Kepler publishes his laws of planetary motion.

1610    Galileo Galilei observes the moons of Jupiter through a telescope.

1628    William Harvey publishes his discovery of the circulation of the blood.

1643    Mercury barometer invented by Evangelista Torricelli.

1656    Christiaan Huygens correctly

identifies the rings of Saturn, and invents the pendulum clock.

1662    The law relating the pressure and volume of a gas discovered by Robert Boyle, and named after him.

1665    Robert Hooke describes living cells.

1668    A functional reflecting telescope is made by Isaac Newton, unaware of Digges's earlier work.

1673    Antony van Leeuwenhoeck reports his discoveries with the microscope to the Royal Society.

1675    Ole Roemer measures the speed of light by timing eclipses of the moons of Jupiter.

1683    Van Leeuwenhoeck observes bacteria.

1687    Publication of Newton's

*Principia*, which includes his law of gravitation.

1705    Edmond Halley publishes his prediction of the return of the comet that now bears his name.

1737    Carl Linnaeus publishes his classification of plants.

1749    Georges Louis Leclerc, Comte de Buffon, defines a species in the modern sense.

1758    Halley's Comet returns, as predicted.

1760    John Michell explains earthquakes.

1772    Carl Scheele discovers oxygen; Joseph Priestley independently discovers it two years later.

1773    Pierre de Laplace begins his work on refining planetary orbits. When asked by Napoleon why there was no mention of God in his scheme, Laplace replied, 'I have no need of that hypothesis.'

1783    John Michell is the first person to suggest the existence of 'dark stars' – now known as black holes.

1789    Antoine Lavoisier publishes a table of thirty-one chemical elements.

1796    Edward Jenner carries out the first inoculation, against smallpox.

1798    Henry Cavendish determines the mass of the Earth.

1802    Thomas Young publishes his first paper on the wave theory of light.
         Jean-Baptiste Lamarck invents the term 'biology'.

1803    John Dalton proposes the atomic theory of matter.

1807    Humphry Davy discovers sodium and potassium, and

|        |                                                                                                    |
|--------|----------------------------------------------------------------------------------------------------|
|        | goes on to find several other elements.                                                            |
| 1811   | Amedeo Avogadro proposes the law that gases contain equal numbers of molecules under the same conditions. |
| 1816   | Augustin Fresnel develops his version of the wave theory of light.                                 |
| 1826   | First photograph from nature obtained by Nicéphore Niépce.                                          |
| 1828   | Friedrich Wöhler synthesizes an organic compound (urea) from inorganic ingredients.                |
| 1830   | Publication of the first volume of Charles Lyell's *Principles of Geology*.                         |
| 1831   | Michael Faraday and Joseph Henry discover electromagnetic induction. Charles Darwin sets sail on the *Beagle*. |
| 1837   | Louis Agassiz coins the term                                                                       |

'ice age' (*die Eiszeit*).

| | |
|---|---|
| 1842 | Christian Doppler describes the effect that now bears his name. |
| 1849 | Hippolyte Fizeau measures the speed of light to within 5 per cent of the modern value. |
| 1851 | Jean Foucault uses his eponymous pendulum to demonstrate the rotation of the Earth. |
| 1857 | Publication of Darwin's *Origin of Species*. Coincidentally, Gregor Mendel begins his experiments with pea breeding. |
| 1864 | James Clerk Maxwell formulates equations describing all electric and magnetic phenomena, and shows that light is an electromagnetic wave. |
| 1868 | Jules Janssen and Norman |

|       | Lockyer identify helium from its lines in the Sun's spectrum. |
|-------|-------------|
| 1871  | Dmitri Mendeleyev predicts that 'new' elements will be found to fit the gaps in his periodic table. |
| 1887  | Experiment carried out by Albert Michelson and Edward Morley finds no evidence for the existence of an 'aether'. |
| 1895  | X-rays discovered by Wilhelm Röntgen. Sigmund Freud begins to develop psychoanalysis. |
| 1896  | Antoine Becquerel discovers radioactivity. |
| 1897  | Electron identified by J. J. Thomson. |
| 1898  | Marie and Pierre Curie discover radium. |
| 1900  | Max Planck explains how electromagnetic radiation is absorbed and emitted as |

quanta. Various biologists rediscover Medel's principles of genetics and heredity.

1903    First powered and controlled flight in an aircraft heavier than air, by Orville Wright.

1905    Einstein's special theory of relativity published.

1908    Hermann Minkowski shows that the special theory of relativity can be elegantly explained in geometrical terms if time is the fourth dimension.

1909    First use of the word 'gene', by Wilhelm Johannsen.

1912    Discovery of cosmic rays by Victor Hess. Alfred Wegener proposes the idea of continental drift, which led in the 1960s to the theory of plate tectonics.

1913    Discovery of the ozone layer by Charles Fabry.

| | |
|---|---|
| 1914 | Ernest Rutherford discovers the proton, a name he coins in 1919. |
| 1915 | Einstein presents his general theory of relativity to the Prussian Academy of Sciences. |
| 1916 | Karl Schwarzschild shows that the general theory of relativity predicts the existence of what are now called black holes. |
| 1919 | Arthur Eddington and others observe the bending of starlight during a total eclipse of the Sun, and so confirm the accuracy of the general theory of relativity. Rutherford splits the atom. |
| 1923 | Louis de Broglie suggests that electrons can behave as waves. |
| 1926 | Enrico Fermi and Paul Dirac discover the statistical rules which govern the behaviour |

of quantum particles such as electrons.

1927     Werner Heisenberg develops the uncertainty principle.

1928     Alexander Fleming discovers penicillin.

1929     Edwin Hubble discovers that the Universe is expanding.

1930s     Linus Pauling explains chemistry in terms of quantum physics.

1932     Neutron discovered by James Chadwick.

1937     Grote Reber builds the first radio telescope.

1942     First controlled nuclear reaction achieved by Enrico Fermi and others.

1940s     George Gamow, Ralph Alpher and Robert Herman develop the Big Bang theory of the origin of the Universe.

1948     Richard Feynman extends quantum theory by

developing quantum electrodynamics.

1951     Francis Crick and James Watson work out the helix structure of DNA, using X-ray results obtained by Rosalind Franklin.

1957     Fred Hoyle, together with William Fowler and Geoffrey and Margaret Burbidge, explains how elements are synthesized inside stars. The laser is devised by Gordon Gould. Launch of first artificial satellite, *Sputnik 1*.

1960     Jacques Monod and Francis Jacob identify messenger RNA.

1961     First part of the genetic code cracked by Marshall Nirenberg.

1963     Discovery of quasars by Maarten Schmidt.

1964     W.D. Hamilton explains

altruism in terms of what is now called sociobiology.

1965    Arno Penzias and Robert Wilson discover the cosmic background radiation left over from the Big Bang.

1967    Discovery of the first pulsar by Jocelyn Bell.

1979    Alan Guth starts to develop the inflationary model of the very early Universe.

1988    Scientists at Caltech discover that there is nothing in the laws of physics that forbids time travel.

1995    Top quark identified.

1996    Tentative identification of evidence of primitive life in a meteorite believed to have originated on Mars.